GREEN EYES

A PLAY IN THREE ACTS

Bare Bones Acting Edition

Based on a play by Clyde Fitch

Revised and edited by Kenneth Stoeffler

Nightsson's Books

Rockport, Massachusetts

2022

I extend loving thanks to the fine people that
make up the community theater om Cape Ann for
the camaraderie and collaboration in making
theater magic.

CHARACTERS:

JINNY AUSTIN nèe Tillman
JOHN "JACK" AUSTIN
MR. THOMAS TILLMAN
MRS. AMELIA TILLMAN
GEOFF TILLMAN, Jinny's brother

RUTH CHESTER, Jinny's best friend
MAGGIE O'RIORDAN, Tillman's servant
MRS. EULALIA SCHRAM, Family friend
PETER SCHRAM, Her son

TIME: 1902
PLACE: New York

ACT I. The Tillmans' House, New York. The Wedding.
 (Two months elapse)
ACT II. The Vatican, Rome. The Honeymoon.
 (Three weeks elapse)
ACT III. The Austin's' House, New York. Home.

Contents

Clyde Fitch

Clara Bloodgood

Green Eyes

Based on a play by Clyde Fitch

Revised and edited by Kenneth Stoeffler

ACT I

SCENE 1

A charming room in the Tillmans' house. The end of May.

ONSTAGE: MAGGIE O'RIORDAN

SFX: GEOFF AND RUTH OUTSIDE DOOR.

EXIT: MAGGIE HIDES BEHIND A DOOR.

ENTER: GEOFF AND RUTH

GEOFF TILLMAN: I want to tell you something. You love me? I love you. That's the important thing.

RUTH CHESTER: Ok. But how much longer must we keep it secret? When will we have our public wedding?

GEOFF TILLMAN: I need to straighten out my affairs. I can't explain it all to you right now. I made a terrible mistake, a kind of debt, while I was at Yale.

RUTH CHESTER: I have a little money.

GEOFF TILLMAN: It isn't a money debt.

RUTH CHESTER: What is it? Let me help. I want to move forward. Everyone was so happy at the wedding today. Jinny was brimming over with joy. I want that. I want a public wedding and joy. I'm tired of hiding and waiting. I want to start a family. I feel ...

GEOFF TILLMAN: I know I'm an ass. I hate myself for all I've done. I hate the pain and trouble I am causing you now. I promise, soon we'll have a house and children.

RUTH CHESTER: I'll leave it alone for now. What's wrong?

GEOFF TILLMAN: I can't forget what I've done. How it's hurting you. How can you love me?

RUTH CHESTER: I do. I just do. You are worth everything to me, and you will be worth much to the world in time. If it hadn't been for you, I wouldn't have learned about operas and plays. I really want to start a family.

GEOFF TILLMAN: I love you, Ruth. More than you will ever know. I don't deserve you. You must know that loving you changed me. It makes those pleasures I indulged in fade away.

RUTH CHESTER: Geoff.

GEOFF TILLMAN: I used to think those pleasures were the only things worth living for. But now, thanks to you, I see a bigger world. I hate that I was so selfish..

RUTH CHESTER: You need me?.

GEOFF TILLMAN: Yes. If I had only met you earlier, I'd be a different man now.

RUTH CHESTER: If you were different, then I might not have fallen in love with you.

GEOFF TILLMAN: The good news is I hope to have things settled in a couple of weeks.

RUTH CHESTER: Geoff.

GEOFF TILLMAN: If I'm not successful, we may have to wait years.

RUTH CHESTER: I couldn't bear it. It's not easy for me to lie. I can't keep it up. It's not fair.

ENTER: PETER

PETER SCHRAM: Here you are.

GEOFF TILLMAN: I'm surprised to see you've left the food table, Peter.

PETER SCHRAM: They sent me to find Miss Chester they're going to cut the bridesmaid's cake and toss the bouquet. Miss Chester, maybe it'll be your lucky day.

RUTH CHESTER: I'd better go.

GEOFF TILLMAN: What's the matter with you?

PETER SCHRAM: I've eaten too much. I've got indigestion. I need a charcoal tablet.

RUTH CHESTER: Come with me and we'll get a glass of water.

PETER SCHRAM: No, it's very bad to drink water with your meals. I'll get a piece of bridesmaid's cake. That'll push it down.

EXIT: PETER AND RUTH

SCENE 2

ENTER: MAGGIE FROM BEHIND DOOR.

GEOFF TILLMAN: What do you want? How long have you been listening?

MAGGIE O'RIORDAN: So that's it, is it? You want to marry her, respectable Miss Ruth Chester, after you can get rid of me. I was only good enough for you to prove your manhood.

GEOFF TILLMAN: No. What do you mean?

MAGGIE O'RIORDAN: I may not have heard everything, but I heard and saw enough to know that you're after her. You won't marry her. I won't let you. I'll never set you free.

GEOFF TILLMAN: What do you want?

MAGGIE O'RIORDAN: When I came to your parent's house as maid, it was because I loved you. You treated me like crap. I hoped by seeing you again, and being near you, you would come back to me and everything would be made right.

GEOFF TILLMAN: Never. Never. It's impossible.

MAGGIE O'RIORDAN: Is it? The dirty little money you give me now only holds my tongue for so long. And you shouldn't be running after any other women. I know your true tastes. The minute you mess with me, the whole town will know it and you can say good-bye to any prospects you have. I'll ruin you.

GEOFF TILLMAN: I was drunk.

MAGGIE O'RIORDAN: You had to be drunk to be with a woman. I know your secret. Remember, I let you prove your manhood. Me.

GEOFF TILLMAN: But I was only twenty. You led me on.

MAGGIE O'RIORDAN: Led you on? I was a decent and nice girl in New Haven doing the housework. You came after me. This is the wedding ring that you put on my finger. You made me respectable, but after the baby died you left me. My mother has the wedding certificate and your daughter's birth and death certificate in a safe place. I led you on? And another thing, I've seen how you have your eyes on the steamer docks still. I know where you go and I know what that means.

GEOFF TILLMAN: We can't talk here.

MAGGIE O'RIORDAN: If I didn't like your sister and your parents I'd just show you what I'm capable of right now. If I lose you, I will still be the poor servant, but you would be destroyed. And you'd take your family with you. Get rid of Miss. Ruth.

GEOFF TILLMAN: I'll buy you off if I can't divorce you.

MAGGIE O'RIORDAN: You? Funny. I don't want your money.

OFFSTAGE: VOICES OF JINNY AND RUTH

GEOFF TILLMAN: Someone's coming.

MAGGIE O'RIORDAN: You haven't got a dime. I know your father gives you the money you give me. I've seen the checks. You have nothing. I'm not going anywhere. So, you better say good-bye to Miss. Ruth. Steamer docks. I've seen you, punk.

EXIT: MAGGIE

GEOFF TILLMAN: Crap.

EXIT: GEOFF

SCENE 3

ENTER: JINNY AND RUTH

JINNY AUSTIN: Not a soul. Come on, follow me. Now that we're alone I wish to say goodbye.

ENTER: JACK

AUSTIN: Hello. May a mere man join this tea party?

JINNY AUSTIN: No, Jack. Wait by the door until I call you.

EXIT: JACK

JINNY AUSTIN: I prepared a little speech. But I've forgotten it. My thoughts have been in a jumble since last week. What I really want to say is: we've known each other since we were climbing apple trees. You're my best friend. Thank you for being my bridesmaid. I truly love you and I couldn't have pulled this off without you. I'm so happy. And ... I want your wedding to be as happy as mine. You must try it. Here's a gift for you.

RUTH CHESTER: Jinny.

JINNY AUSTIN: I'll be home in October, if you aren't engaged to be married by then, I'll wash my hands of you. Jack! You can come in now.

JACK AUSTIN: All the guests have gone …. Have you been crying?

JINNY AUSTIN: No.

JACK AUSTIN: Come on now. All the guests have gone except the Schrams, who are upstairs with your mother looking at the presents. Your mother asked for you. And I've been ordered by my father-in-law to go to my room and dress now. He's worried we will miss our train.

RUTH CHESTER: Jack.

JACK AUSTIN: Yes.

RUTH CHESTER: You like your new brother, don't you?

JACK AUSTIN: Geoff? Most certainly I do, and Jinny adores him.

RUTH CHESTER: I know, then, you'll be a good friend to him if he needs one.

JACK AUSTIN: Of course.

RUTH CHESTER: I think he really needs one now.

JACK AUSTIN: Really?

RUTH CHESTER: Please don't tell anyone, not even Jinny. I may be betraying something I've no right to do. Please don't tell him I've spoken to you. I just want to help him.

JACK AUSTIN: All right.

RUTH CHESTER: Thank you.

JACK AUSTIN: Goodbye.

RUTH CHESTER: Goodbye, Jinny. I love you. Have a fantastic honeymoon.

EXIT: RUTH

JINNY AUSTIN: Goodbye .... What were you two talking about?

JACK AUSTIN: Goodbyes.

JINNY AUSTIN: Do you know what I believe? Ruth Chester's in love with you. That explains the whole thing. *Pas étonnant qu'elle ait été si triste aujourd'hui.*

JACK AUSTIN: What?

JINNY AUSTIN: I said, "No wonder she was so sad today." Jack you really need to brush up on your French.

JACK AUSTIN: I understood the French. I was questioning your absurd notion that Ruth loves me.

JINNY AUSTIN: I know it's not your fault. There was no other woman in this house for you today but me, was there?

JACK AUSTIN: There was no other woman in the world for me since the first day I met you.

JINNY AUSTIN: Goodbye, Jinny Tillman. Do you think I could sit on your knee like a little child and put my arm around your neck and rest my head on your shoulder for just five seconds. I'm so tired.

SCENE 4

MRS. EULALIA SCHRAM: Excuse me.

JINNY AUSTIN: No, come in.

MRS. EULALIA SCHRAM: I'm sorry to interrupt you, but I just wanted to say goodbye. Peter.

PETER SCHRAM: Yes mother.

JACK AUSTIN: I'm much obliged to you, Mrs. Schram, for the interruption, as I was sent long ago to make myself ready for the train, if you'll excuse me.

MRS. EULALIA SCHRAM: Certainly.

MRS. EULALIA SCHRAM: If it's time for him, it's certainly time for you. I won't keep you a minute.

JINNY AUSTIN: And isn't Jack so handsome.

MRS. EULALIA SCHRAM: He is. And so are you. In fact, I've been telling your mother I don't know how to thank you both. You've asked me today to meet the swellest crowd I've ever had chance to rub elbows with. And I didn't have to buy tickets for the invitation. I was really, able, to converse with them besides "excuse me," and "I beg your pardon." Of course, I've sat next to them all before in restaurants and at concerts, but this time it felt like the real thing. Like I was accepted in New York society. I shall never forget it.

JINNY AUSTIN: I'm so happy to know that you had a good time. Please don't feel indebted to us. Ever since we met you in Egypt that winter, mamma, and I knew right away that we would be best friends.

MRS. EULALIA SCHRAM: Thank you.

[PETER FARTS]

MRS. EULALIA SCHRAM: Peter.

PETER: Excuse me.

MRS. EULALIA SCHRAM: He suffers terribly from indigestion. That's the alkali powder he takes twenty minutes after eating. Peter, we must say goodbye now.

PETER SCHRAM: Goodbye, Miss Jinny.

MRS. EULALIA SCHRAM: Peter, it's Mrs. Austin now.

JINNY AUSTIN: I can always be "Miss Jinny" to you Peter.

PETER SCHRAM: Thank you. I had a great time. The food was great, but I'm feeling it now. [FARTS] Excuse me.

MRS. EULALIA SCHRAM: I was just telling Mrs. Austin

JINNY AUSTIN: Please call me Jinny. Nothing's changed between us.

MRS. EULALIA SCHRAM: Thank you. I was just saying we won't forget you in our social life. Will we, Peter? Now that Miss Jinny gave us the biggest boost [PETER FARTS] we've had yet.

PETER SCHRAM: Well, you know, mother, I don't think the game is worth the candle. It's begun to pall on me already.

MRS. EULALIA SCHRAM: I really think he's going to be superior to it.

PETER SCHRAM: I only go now for your sake.

ENTER: MRS. TILLMAN

MRS. AMELIA TILLMAN: Jinny. Jinny.

JINNY AUSTIN: Mother. I ought to dress.

MRS. AMELIA TILLMAN: She'll be late if she isn't careful.

JINNY AUSTIN: I'm going.

MRS. AMELIA TILLMAN: Hurry.

EXIT: JINNY

MRS. AMELIA TILLMAN: Come, I want to give you some of Jinny's flowers to take home with you. Would you like some?

MRS. EULALIA SCHRAM: I would love them.

EXIT: MRS. TILLMAN, MRS. SCHRAM, AND PETER.

SCENE 5

ENTER: MAGGIE AND AUSTIN

MAGGIE O'RIORDAN: I beg pardon, sir, but may I speak to you a minute?

JACK AUSTIN: Certainly, Maggie, what is it?

MAGGIE O'RIORDAN: I've been trying for a chance to see you alone. I wouldn't bother you. sir. It's because I'm fond of Miss. Jinny … I mean, Mrs. Austin, and of Mr. and Mrs. Tillman. They've all been so good to me. I know it would nearly kill them if they knew.

JACK AUSTIN: Knew what?

MAGGIE O'RIORDAN: Well, one member of this family hasn't been good to me, sir. He's been bad. Bad as he could be. And somebody's got to talk to him, and I don't see who's going to do it but you. If he don't change, I'll not hold my tongue any longer. It's all I can do for their sakes to hold it now.

JACK AUSTIN: Geoff?

MAGGIE O'RIORDAN: Yes, sir. He's my husband.

JACK AUSTIN: What?

MAGGIE O'RIORDAN: We were married when he was at Yale, sir. I was in a shop there and I cleaned the frat house on the side. He lived there.

JACK AUSTIN: Why bring me in on this?

MAGGIE O'RIORDAN: Because he's courting Miss. Chester and promising to marry her. And if he doesn't stop I'll make trouble.

JACK AUSTIN: But if he's married to you, as you say, he can't marry anyone else.

MAGGIE O'RIORDAN: I know. He's tried to make me believe our marriage isn't legal, because he was only twenty and had been drinking.

JACK AUSTIN: What makes you think Geoff cares for Miss. Chester?

MAGGIE O'RIORDAN: I've seen them together. They were holding hands and kissing. And I heard him tell her.

JACK AUSTIN: What? Anything more?

MAGGIE O'RIORDAN: I love him, sir, even if I'm only a servant. I can't stand to think he's going to try and get rid of me for someone else.

JACK AUSTIN: Here, sit down a minute. Calm down. They'll be coming down soon. I'll have a talk with Geoff when I come back.

ENTER: GEOFF

GEOFF TILLMAN: Thank goodness I've caught you. I had an awful headache and went out for a breath of air. I think I'll need a headache powder. I was afraid I missed you. Jinny would never forgive me. Maggie?

JACK AUSTIN: Geoff, is what Maggie just told me true?

GEOFF TILLMAN: What did she tell you?

JACK AUSTIN: That you married her in New Haven?

GEOFF TILLMAN: Yes.

MRS. TILLMAN: [OFFSTAGE] Maggie.

MAGGIE O'RIORDAN: I'll go.

EXIT: MAGGIE

GEOFF TILLMAN: Promise me, Jack, you won't tell anyone. For two years at college I went all to pieces and led a rotten life, and one night, drunk, I married her. It isn't her fault. I suppose she thought I loved her. But this would hurt my parents if they knew. And Jinny, for God's sake, don't tell Jinny. She respects me. Please don't tell her.

JACK AUSTIN: I won't. But Maggie says you want to marry someone else now.

GEOFF TILLMAN: That's true.

JACK AUSTIN: How are you going to do it?

GEOFF TILLMAN: I must make money somehow and buy off Maggie.

JACK AUSTIN: You can go out to Sioux Falls for a no-fault divorce and make a settlement on respectable grounds.

GEOFF TILLMAN: I can't do that.

JACK AUSTIN: Why not?

GEOFF TILLMAN: I can't do anything publicly.

JACK AUSTIN: You can't avoid it. There's no other way around it.

GEOFF TILLMAN: I can't have publicity it would kill Ruth.

JACK AUSTIN: If she loves you, she'll forgive your wild oats, especially as everyone sees now what a steady, straight fellow you've become.

GEOFF TILLMAN: I can't do that to her. No. Jack, please help. You will, won't you? Do it for Jinny's sake. Help me to persuade Maggie to keep silent for good. Have her tear up the marriage certificate. I was only twenty. It's hardly legal. And I'll give a good sum to go away.

JACK AUSTIN: You're proposing bigamy? You've done enough. Don't stoop to crime. Forget you ever said that. Do what I tell you. When Jinny and I have gone abroad, you must go to Sioux Falls. If you need money, let me know.

ENTER: JINNY

JINNY AUSTIN: Ready. And there you are, Geoff. I've been sending the servants all over the house after you. Goodbye brother. Haven't we had good times together since childhood, except that time you put a crab in my bed at the Parkinson Hotel on Fire Island. I'll miss you, but not the crabs. I used to think I'd never marry at all if I couldn't marry you. I know that's silly now, but I really did feel that way back then. But then Jack came along and swept me off my feet. He's the only one who could have done that. Is that jealousy I see?

JACK AUSTIN: No.

JINNY AUSTIN: Isn't it awful. You can't make him jealous. I think it's an absolutely positive flaw in his character. He's not like us, is he? And I know you've overcome certain things, Geoff. I know it's been hard, and I'm proud of you.

GEOFF TILLMAN: The house will be quiet without you. I'll miss you.

EXIT: GEOFF

JINNY AUSTIN: He's going to cry. Jack, you'll be a brother to Geoff, won't you?

JACK AUSTIN: I'll be there for him Jinny. He is my brother now.

JINNY AUSTIN: Thank you. Wait here just a minute. I know he won't come back to say goodbye. I'll go up to his room. It's almost like the games we played as children.

ENTER: MR. and MRS. TILLMAN

MR. THOMAS TILLMAN: The carriage is here.

JINNY AUSTIN: I won't be a second.

EXIT: JINNY

MRS. AMELIA TILLMAN: Where is she going?

JACK AUSTIN: Up to her brother.

MRS. AMELIA TILLMAN: Her father's been locked in his study for three hours. He told me he was thinking. But his eyes look very suspicious.

MR. THOMAS TILLMAN: Nonsense.

MRS. AMELIA TILLMAN: How many cigars did you smoke?

MR. THOMAS TILLMAN: Eight.

MRS. AMELIA TILLMAN: The amount of emotion that a man can soak out of himself with tobacco is wonderful. He uses it just like a sponge.

MR. THOMAS TILLMAN: Jack, the first thing I asked about you when I heard that, that things were getting this way, was, does he smoke? A man who smokes always has that outlet. If things go wrong, go out and smoke a cigar. And when the cigar's finished, ten to one everything's got right, somehow. If you lose your temper, don't speak, smoke a cigar. And, when it's finished, then speak. You'll find the temper has gone up with the smoke. A woman's happiness is safest with a man who smokes. God bless you, Jack, it is a wrench. Jinny's our only girl, you know. She's been a great joy.

MRS. AMELIA TILLMAN: No, no, they're going now.

MR. THOMAS TILLMAN: The best I can say is, I wish you as happy a married life as we've had.

MRS. AMELIA TILLMAN: Thirty-five years.

MR. THOMAS TILLMAN: Thirty-five wonderful years. But there is one rift Jack. Little threads of jealousy have snapped our happiness sometimes.

MRS. AMELIA TILLMAN: Nothing ever serious of course, but it's a fault that Jinny shares with us.

MR. THOMAS TILLMAN: We called her Greenie. 'The girl with the green eyes'. Sometimes her jealousy was pretty strong.

MRS. AMELIA TILLMAN: You'll always bear with her, won't you, even if her jealousy flares?

JACK AUSTIN: I'll never give her the chance to be jealous.

MRS. AMELIA TILLMAN: It isn't a question of chance. You just can't help it sometimes. Isn't that right, George?

JACK AUSTIN: Don't worry. Your daughter's safe with me. I'm not the jealous sort myself and I love Jinny so completely, so calmly with my heart, soul, body, and mind. She'll never have a chance even to try to be jealous of me.

ENTER: JINNY

JINNY AUSTIN: I found poor Maggie up in my room crying. I think she's having second thoughts about not accepting our invitation to be our maid on the trip. I also said goodbye to cook. And he sniffed too.

JACK AUSTIN: We ought to go.

MRS. AMELIA TILLMAN: Goodbye, darling.

JINNY AUSTIN: Goodbye, father. Mommy, I shall miss you. You'll send me a letter tomorrow, won't you, or a telegram? Send a telegram. You've got the address, right?

MRS. AMELIA TILLMAN: Yes, it's written down.

MR. THOMAS TILLMAN: Come, Harriet. They'll lose their train.

JINNY AUSTIN: Goodbye, mother.

MRS. AMELIA TILLMAN: Goodbye. And don't overindulge. And write me back every day.

MR. THOMAS TILLMAN: Hurry, they'll lose their train.

JINNY AUSTIN: Jack.

JACK AUSTIN: Jinny, Jinny, you're not sorry, are you?

JINNY AUSTIN: Sorry? No. It hurts me to leave them, but I've never been so happy in my life.

EXIT: JACK AND JINNY

SFX: CARRIAGE DOOR CLOSING AND HORSE STEPS

MR. THOMAS TILLMAN: There they go.

ACT II

SCENE 1

The Vatican, Rome. The *Tribune of the Apollo Belvedere*. A semicircular room with dark red walls. In the center is the large statue of Apollo.

[Two months later]

ONSTAGE: JINNY AND AUSTIN

JINNY AUSTIN: What do you keep looking at, Jackie?

JACK AUSTIN: I thought I saw someone I know.

JINNY AUSTIN: Who?

JACK AUSTIN: I don't know. From behind they just seemed familiar. It was their movements. Anyway.

JINNY AUSTIN: I think the present works of art, and your loving wife are quite enough for you to look at without hunting around for familiar backs.

JACK AUSTIN: And Baedeker. [Reading] Apollo Belvedere, found at the end of the fifteenth century, probably in a Roman villa.

JINNY AUSTIN: Of course. Apollo.

JACK AUSTIN: Great, isn't it?

JINNY AUSTIN: Stunning. Still, I suppose I'm prejudiced.

JACK AUSTIN: What?

JINNY AUSTIN: You old stupid fool. You know, Jack, you're deeply and fundamentally clever and brilliant, but you're not quite bright, not quick.

JACK AUSTIN: Don't you think having one in the family is enough? What have I missed this time, Jinny? You don't mean you've found a family likeness in the statue over there? I don't want to be unappreciative, but it doesn't suggest your father to me in the least, nor even Geoff.

JINNY AUSTIN: It doesn't suggest anybody to me, I was only thinking I sympathize with Mrs. Perkins of Boston, don't you know the story about her?

JACK AUSTIN: No, what is it?

JINNY AUSTIN: Mrs. Perkins from Boston was personally conducted here and shown this very statue. She looked at it for a few moments, and then turned around and said, "Yes, it's all right, but give me Mr. Perkins anytime."

JACK AUSTIN: Jinny.

JINNY AUSTIN: Are you shocked? Come, I'm tired. Let's sit down here and I'll read my letters. Here's one from Geoff.

JACK AUSTIN: I'll read ahead in Baedeker and you tell me if there's any news. Where is Geoff's letter from?

JINNY AUSTIN: New York, where else would it be?

JACK AUSTIN: I thought he was going away on a trip.

JINNY AUSTIN: Where?

JACK AUSTIN: West, somewhere.

JINNY AUSTIN: But why would he go West?

JACK AUSTIN: He had some business, I believe. I remember thinking it was a good idea when he told me. It was the day we were married. I was waiting for you to come downstairs.

JINNY AUSTIN: That's funny. Geoff never said anything to me.

JACK AUSTIN: You were busy getting married.

JINNY AUSTIN: I was.

JACK AUSTIN: By the way, when you answer your brother's letter, tell him I seemed surprised he was still in New York.

JINNY AUSTIN: Um ok. What do you think?

JACK AUSTIN: That you're the sweetest woman in the world.

JINNY AUSTIN: No, I mean, guess who Geoff says is here in Italy?

JACK AUSTIN: I have no idea. As far as I'm concerned, there is no one in Italy but you and me.

JINNY AUSTIN: If you keep on talking like that, I shall kiss you.

JACK AUSTIN: What. Before Apollo? I'm dumbfounded.

JINNY AUSTIN: Silly. It seems Mrs. Schram and Peter brought Ruth here.

JACK AUSTIN: Then it was her back.

JINNY AUSTIN: What?

JACK AUSTIN: That I saw just now.

JINNY AUSTIN: You said you didn't know who it reminded you of.

JACK AUSTIN: I know, I didn't until you mentioned her.

JINNY AUSTIN: But if you thought it was Ruth Chester, why didn't you say so then?

JACK AUSTIN: I simply didn't think of her at the time.

JINNY AUSTIN: Well next time think.

JACK AUSTIN: What else does Geoff say?

JINNY AUSTIN: Nothing. There was horrible heat for two days. Already they miss me more than he can tell me.

JACK AUSTIN: I bet.

JINNY AUSTIN: Father constantly smoked cigars the first week I was gone.

JACK AUSTIN: I haven't had to smoke any.

JINNY AUSTIN: Mercy. Don't boast. And he thinks they will soon all go to Long Island for the summer.

JACK AUSTIN: And he doesn't mention going West?

JINNY AUSTIN: No, he says he may go to Newport for August, and that's all. Why do you care so much if he's going West or not?

JACK AUSTIN: Going to read all those?

JINNY AUSTIN: If you don't mind. Do you mind?

JACK AUSTIN: No. While you're reading, I'll go look for the Schrams.

JINNY AUSTIN: Ok.

JACK AUSTIN: If I find them, I'll bring them here.

EXIT: JACK

SCENE 2

ENTER: MRS. SCHRAM

MRS. EULALIA SCHRAM: Jinny?

JINNY AUSTIN: Mrs. Schram. Did Jack find you?

MRS. EULALIA SCHRAM: No, we haven't seen him. Ruth and Peter are dawdling along, each on their own. I like to shoot through a gallery. There's no use spending so much time. When it's over, you've mixed everything up anyway. It's all just the same.

JINNY AUSTIN: I just read a letter from Geoff saying you were over here. And Jack, who thought he got a glimpse of you a little while ago, went straight off to find you.

MRS. EULALIA SCHRAM: What fun it is to see you and how happy you look.

JINNY AUSTIN: I can't look as happy as I feel.

MRS. EULALIA SCHRAM: Who's your friend? Nice gent, isn't he?

JINNY AUSTIN: Mr. Apollo. Would you like to meet him?

MRS. EULALIA SCHRAM: Er, no, I don't think so. You must draw the line somewhere. He wouldn't stand up to Corbett, would he?

JINNY AUSTIN: Who's Corbett?

MRS. EULALIA SCHRAM: He was a prize fighter and was...but that's another story. You've never heard of him?

JINNY AUSTIN: The name sounds familiar. But this is Apollo. The god Apollo.

MRS. EULALIA SCHRAM: No, I don't know. Was he a champion?

JINNY AUSTIN: No, he was a Greek god.

MRS. EULALIA SCHRAM: Was he? Well, I wouldn't have cared about being in the tailoring business in those days? How'd they make money? Let's sit down. You know, in Peoria, where I come from, we would never accept a thing like that as a gift. No, indeed. If the King of Italy sent it to our Mayor, he'd return it C.O.D.

JINNY AUSTIN: Sounds like Boston and MacMonnies' *Bacchante and Infant Faun* statue.

MRS. EULALIA SCHRAM: Worse than that. It reminds me of a man Mr. Jones, who kept an underclothing store on Main street. He had a plaster cast of his brother … well I think it was his brother, in his window to display a suit of Jaegers. You know, a "combination". And our Town Committee of Thirteen, for the moral improvement of Peoria, made Mr. Jones take it out of his window. It was a little to realistic, if you know what I mean. You ought to see our Park. You know we've got a perfectly beautiful park, and all the men statues are smartly dressed, and stand like this, as if they were saying, "This way out" or "This way to the lion cage and zoo."

JINNY AUSTIN: And the women statues?

MRS. EULALIA SCHRAM: They only have heads and hands. All the rest is just clumps of drapery. We only have "Americans" and "Liberties," anyway. They apply the Chinese emigration law to all Venuses and such ladies.

JINNY AUSTIN: Where did you say Peter and Ruth were?

MRS. EULALIA SCHRAM: I left Peter, who isn't at all well. I hoped this trip would help his indigestion, but it seems to have made it worse. I left him in a room with a lot of broken-up Venuses. I thought it was all right. He was eating candy, and there wasn't a whole woman among them.

JINNY AUSTIN: How did you happen to bring Ruth Chester with you?

MRS. EULALIA SCHRAM: I've always liked her. She never snubbed me. And no one has been as nice to Peter and me as Mrs. Chester and Ruth. Except for you and our mother to be sure.

JINNY AUSTIN: They are genuinely nice people.

MRS. EULALIA SCHRAM: Ruth is terribly depressed. She's thin as a rail and the family is worried. She says there's nothing, and the doctors can't find anything wrong. So Mrs. Chester asked me if I wouldn't take her abroad. They thought the voyage and change might do her good. I seem to have a cheerier influence over her than most people. So here we are. There's Peter.

ENTER: PETER

PETER SCHRAM: How do you do, Mrs. Austin?

JINNY AUSTIN: How are you, Peter? I'm sorry to hear you're sick. You eat too many sweet things.

PETER SCHRAM: I'm not eating candy. It's soda mints. It's bad today, mother. [FARTS]

MRS. EULALIA SCHRAM: If you don't get better, we'll go to Carlsbad.

JINNY AUSTIN: How do you like Rome, Peter?

PETER SCHRAM: I don't know. Too much Boston and not enough Chicago to make it a real lively town.

JINNY AUSTIN: I'm going to go look for Jack and tell him you've turned up.

MRS. EULALIA SCHRAM: Perhaps he's found Ruth.

JINNY AUSTIN: Yes, perhaps.

PETER SCHRAM: Ruth's in a room on your left, with rows of men's heads on shelves. Emperors, and things.

EXIT: JINNY

MRS. EULALIA SCHRAM: Isn't it beautiful, Peter?

PETER SCHRAM: No, it's too big.

MRS. EULALIA SCHRAM: Still this one isn't broken.

PETER SCHRAM: It's been mended, too. But it's only another of these second-hand statues. You missed one whole one. The best I've seen yet. A Venus that was off in a little room, with mosaics, and painted walls, that's where I've been.

MRS. EULALIA SCHRAM: What kind of a Venus?

PETER SCHRAM: I forgot to take my medicine.

MRS. EULALIA SCHRAM: Was she dressed?

PETER SCHRAM: She had been, but she'd sort of pushed it off.

MRS. EULALIA SCHRAM: You know we ought to admire these things. That's partly why we've come to Europe to be educated and cultured. But really.

PETER SCHRAM: Let's go. I'll show you the Venus.

MRS. EULALIA SCHRAM: But Ruth and Mrs. Austin?

PETER SCHRAM: We didn't agree to wait. We can all meet up at the hotel.

EXIT: MRS. SCHRAM AND PETER

SCENE 3

ENTER: JACK AND RUTH

JACK AUSTIN: This is where I left her with Apollo. Jinny. She's gone.

RUTH CHESTER: Mrs. Schram probably found her. She was headed in this direction when I last saw her. They must be looking for us now.

JACK AUSTIN: Let's sit here and wait for them. I'm sorry to hear you've been ill.

RUTH CHESTER: It's nothing.

JACK AUSTIN: Will you forgive me if I say I think I know what it is. You told me that Geoff needed a friend and I've spoken with him.

RUTH CHESTER: I hoped you'd forgotten. I shouldn't to asked you.

JACK AUSTIN: Why not? He told me everything.

RUTH CHESTER: He did. You are sure?

JACK AUSTIN: Yes.

RUTH CHESTER: That he and I...

JACK AUSTIN: Love each other.

RUTH CHESTER: But that isn't all.

JACK AUSTIN: I know the rest too.

RUTH CHESTER: He told you about ...about...

JACK AUSTIN: The marriage. Yes.

RUTH CHESTER: I'm so glad, so glad. Now I can speak of it to someone. I am so unhappy.

JACK AUSTIN: I already advised him, but he doesn't seem to be taking my advice. It worries me.

RUTH CHESTER: When I left, he was awfully depressed too. He said he saw no prospect of being able to publish our marriage for years, maybe.

JACK AUSTIN: What marriage?

RUTH CHESTER: Our marriage. He married me in Brooklyn. You said he told you everything.

JACK AUSTIN: Yes, but not the details. I'm a little confused. I know I should have gone through the details with him, but there wasn't time.

RUTH CHESTER: I can't go on like this much longer. It's killing me to deceive mother. I must tell her soon.

JACK AUSTIN: No. You mustn't, not yet. Can I give you advice?

RUTH CHESTER: Yes. Please help us.

JACK AUSTIN: Where were you and Geoff married?

RUTH CHESTER: In Brooklyn. The Old Brick Church.

JACK AUSTIN: When?

RUTH CHESTER: A month before your wedding. I lied to my mother that day for the first time since I was a child and I've been lying to her ever since.

JACK AUSTIN: But why did you marry so secretly? What was his reason?

RUTH CHESTER: We couldn't afford to marry and set up house for ourselves. And he expected to be sent off at once to the Philippines and he didn't want to leave me behind, free. I'm afraid he's rather jealous. You must have found out by now that Jinny is too. They all are. And I didn't want him to go away without him belonging to me either. I guess I'm jealous too. That's why.

JACK AUSTIN: And this long period of secrecy since then? How does he explain that?

RUTH CHESTER: His debts. Didn't he tell you that? You know before he loved me, he was very irresponsible, but since....

JACK AUSTIN: Yes, I know he gave up his old habits, with courage.

RUTH CHESTER: How can you help us? Can you get him a job so he can pay off his debts? Can you convince him it is better to declare our marriage publicly even if we have to live in separate houses until we can afford our own?

JACK AUSTIN: I'll return to New York, if I can persuade Jinny.

RUTH CHESTER: Me too?

JACK AUSTIN: No. You must stay here until I send word for you to come home. If I am going to help you, you must listen to me.

RUTH CHESTER: I will.

ENTER: JINNY

RUTH CHESTER: Jinny.

JACK AUSTIN: I didn't hear you, Jinny.

JINNY AUSTIN: No, you both seemed so absorbed.

RUTH CHESTER: I'm so glad to see you.

JINNY AUSTIN: Thank you, I just left the Schrams. They told me they were going back to the hotel and would wait for you there.

RUTH CHESTER: Then, I mustn't keep them waiting. Will we meet for dinner tonight?

JINNY AUSTIN: Sure.

EXIT: RUTH

SCENE 4

JINNY AUSTIN: That wasn't true, what I told her I haven't seen the Schrams, and I don't know where they are, and what's more, I don't care.

JACK AUSTIN: What do you mean?

JINNY AUSTIN: What did she mean by following you to Rome?

JACK AUSTIN: Jinny.

JINNY AUSTIN: Don't deny it. That'll only make me suspect you more.

JACK AUSTIN: You don't know what you're saying.

JINNY AUSTIN: They say she's ill. And they don't know what's wrong with her. Yes. No. I can tell them. She's in love with another woman's husband.

JACK AUSTIN: I won't allow you to say such things.

JINNY AUSTIN: Won't you? You'd better be careful. My eyes are open now.

JACK AUSTIN: Yes, and much too wide.

JINNY AUSTIN: A half-blind person would have known there was something between you two. When I came into this room just now, it was thick in the air. It was on both your faces.

JACK AUSTIN: You've worked yourself up to such a pitch you don't know what you're saying.

JINNY AUSTIN: I'm not responsible? What was it she said to you when I entered? I saw your faces. She told you she loved you. She confessed she followed you over here.

JACK AUSTIN: Absolutely false, both your suppositions.

JINNY AUSTIN: Of course you'll protect her. You're a gentleman. But if I thought you knew she was coming over, I'd....

JACK AUSTIN: How can you think that?

JINNY AUSTIN: Why didn't you tell me when you thought you saw her a little while ago? Why didn't you?

JACK AUSTIN: I told you I didn't recognize her. I only thought something familiar flashed across my eyes. Jinny darling, this is sheer madness on your part. It has no reason. It has no excuse. Ask your own heart, and your own mind, if in speaking to me as you have, you haven't done me at least an injustice and my love for you a little wrong.

JINNY AUSTIN: I'm sure she's in love with you, anyway.

JACK AUSTIN: No, she isn't. It's disgraceful of you to say so. I know she isn't.

JINNY AUSTIN: How do you know she isn't?

JACK AUSTIN: There's no question of it. I'm sure of it. You mustn't think just because you love me everybody else does.

JINNY AUSTIN: You're so modest you don't see. But I do. On the steamer, in the hotels, everywhere we go, always, all the women admire you awfully. I see it.

JACK AUSTIN: What utter nonsense. You've got something in your eyes.

JINNY AUSTIN: Only tears.

JACK AUSTIN: No, something else, something green.

JINNY AUSTIN: Somebody's told you my old nickname.

JACK AUSTIN: What?

JINNY AUSTIN: Greenie. I don't care if it is appropriate, I can't help it.

JACK AUSTIN: You must, or it will threaten our happiness if you let yourself be carried away by jealousy for no earthly reason outside of your imagination. Like you have this time.

JINNY AUSTIN: You honestly don't think she cares for you?

JACK AUSTIN: Not a bit.

JINNY AUSTIN: But what was it you were so serious about? What's between you?

JACK AUSTIN: She is in a little trouble, and I happen to know about it.

JINNY AUSTIN: How?

JACK AUSTIN: You mustn't ask me. She didn't tell me, someone else told me.

JINNY AUSTIN: Truly?

JACK AUSTIN: Truly.

JINNY AUSTIN: I don't care. She had no business going to you. She should have gone to a woman for sympathy. She's got Mrs. Schram. Why did she go to you?

JACK AUSTIN: She can't go to her. Mrs. Schram knows nothing about it.

JINNY AUSTIN: Now don't get too sympathetic that's very dangerous.

JACK AUSTIN: Look, your imagination is peeping through the keyhole.

JINNY AUSTIN: What is her trouble, Jack?

JACK AUSTIN: I can't tell you now. Someday, perhaps, if you want me to, but not now. Only I give you my word of honor, it has nothing to do with our relationship. It does not touch our life. And I want you to believe me and trust me. You don't need to be jealous.

JINNY AUSTIN: I do believe you. And I do trust you. And I will try not to be jealous again.

JACK AUSTIN: Thank you.

JINNY AUSTIN: You know that book of De Maupassant's I was reading on the train the other day, about the young girl who killed herself with charcoal fumes when her lover deserted her?

JACK AUSTIN: What's this got to do with it? I have absolutely no sympathy with such people.

JINNY AUSTIN: In America that girl would have simply turned on the gas.

JACK AUSTIN: You're getting morbid.

JINNY AUSTIN: No, I'm not. But if I ever. . .

JACK AUSTIN: I shall install electric light as soon as we get home.

JINNY AUSTIN: I'm sorry I was so disagreeable to Ruth. But I'll try to make up for it in every way I can.

JACK AUSTIN: There's one other thing, Jinny, I'd like to speak of now. Would you mind giving up the Lakes and going home this week?

JINNY AUSTIN: Going home at once?

JACK AUSTIN: Yes Wall Street is very uncertain. I'm worried. And I want to see Geoff about his business.

JINNY AUSTIN: Jack. You're not running away from her, are you?

JACK AUSTIN: Jinny, what did we just talk about?.

JINNY AUSTIN: I'm joking. I'm ready to go back home. I've seen the Lakes. Whether we are in Italy or New York, as long as we are together, it's our honeymoon just the same.

JACK AUSTIN: And may it last all our lives.

JINNY AUSTIN: Still, I don't mind owning up that leaving Ruth Chester behind here is rather pleasanter. She's not returning, is she?

JACK AUSTIN: No. They are over here indefinitely.

JINNY AUSTIN: I've been too horrid and nasty for words this morning, Jack. I'm sorry.

JACK AUSTIN: It's over and forgotten now.

JINNY AUSTIN: You do forgive me?

JACK AUSTIN: Of course, only I want to say this to you. I love you. But this jealousy of yours, based on unfounded suspicions insults me. Insults our relationship.

JINNY AUSTIN: I didn't really suspect you.

JACK AUSTIN: Ok, But it is possible to insult a true love too often. And love can die.

JINNY AUSTIN: Please, don't say any more. You have forgiven me, haven't you?

JACK AUSTIN: Yes.

JINNY AUSTIN: Then kiss me.

JACK AUSTIN: Here. Someone will see us.

JINNY AUSTIN: No, only Apollo. Look, there's no one else here, it's lunchtime.

JACK AUSTIN: But.

JINNY AUSTIN: Come along, then, behind the statue. No one will see us there.

JINNY AUSTIN: There. No one saw us, and I'm so happy, are you?

JACK AUSTIN: Very.

JINNY AUSTIN: Are my eyes still green?

JACK AUSTIN: Now they're blue.

JINNY AUSTIN: Hurrah! And I'm going to be so good from now on. You won't recognize me.

ACT III

SCENE 1

The Austin's library. Two weeks later.

ONSTAGE: MRS. TILLMAN (playing the Sextette from *Floradora*, "*Tell me, Pretty Maiden*" on the player piano)

ENTER: JINNY (singing)

JINNY AUSTIN: Mother.

MRS. AMELIA TILLMAN: I really must get one of these sewing-machine pianos for your father. I believe even he could play it, and it would be lots of fun for us.

JINNY AUSTIN: Jack adores it. I gave it to him for an anniversary present.

MRS. AMELIA TILLMAN: What anniversary?

JINNY AUSTIN: Day before yesterday. The eleventh Tuesday since our marriage. Have you been in town all day? I am so glad to see you. I've been so lonely and bored since we returned. Everyone is in the country.

MRS. AMELIA TILLMAN: Yes, and I told your father to meet me here and we'd take the six-thirty train from Long Island City.

JINNY AUSTIN: Jack and I are going to the theater tonight.

MRS. AMELIA TILLMAN: I thought they were all closed.

JINNY AUSTIN: No, there are several musical comedies playing. Jack's favorite form of amusement. And I bought the tickets myself for his birthday present.

MRS. AMELIA TILLMAN: Is it his birthday?

JINNY AUSTIN: No, that's only my excuse.

MRS. AMELIA TILLMAN: Had we known you and Jack were coming home in August, your father and I wouldn't have gone into the country so late.

JINNY AUSTIN: We've been home two weeks.

MRS. AMELIA TILLMAN: And you're still ideally happy aren't you, darling?

JINNY AUSTIN: Yes.

MRS. AMELIA TILLMAN: Jinny, what does that mean?

JINNY AUSTIN: It's all my horrid disposition.

MRS. AMELIA TILLMAN: Been seeing green?

JINNY AUSTIN: Once in Rome … and on the boat … and again since we've been back.

MRS. AMELIA TILLMAN: Nothing serious?

JINNY AUSTIN: No, but the last time Jack was harder to bring around than before. And he looked at me for a full five minutes without a particle of love in his eyes. They were almost dead eyes.

MRS. AMELIA TILLMAN: What was it all about?

JINNY AUSTIN: Ruth Chester. Mostly.

MRS. AMELIA TILLMAN: Ruth?

JINNY AUSTIN: The first real scene I made was in Rome in the Vatican. I was jealous of her. I can't explain it all to you as a matter of fact. It hasn't all been explained to me. Something was troubling Ruth, Jack knew, and he said he'd help her.

MRS. AMELIA TILLMAN: What?

JINNY AUSTIN: That's just it. Jack won't tell me. And the day we sailed from Naples a telegram came, and of course I opened it, and it said, "Trust me, I will do everything you say. Ruth."

MRS. AMELIA TILLMAN: Why haven't you told me or your father any of this before?

JINNY AUSTIN: I was ashamed. Somehow, in the end I knew I was wrong and had hurt him terribly. Mother, I hurt the man I love better than anything else in the world. Yes. Even better than you and father and Geoff all together.

MRS. AMELIA TILLMAN: This curse of jealousy. I was hoping he was strong enough to help you overcome it.

JINNY AUSTIN: He does try hard. But he hasn't a spark of it in himself and doesn't understand it. I know I'm unreasonable. Before I know it, I am saying things …. I don't know what. Some day he won't forgive me. I'm sure some day he won't.

MRS. AMELIA TILLMAN: Come now, you're getting yourself bent out of shape, and that won't do you any good. You've got to fight this battle out by yourself. You must trust in the deep love of your husband and hope for tolerance. My troubles with your father were never very big because we shared the curse, so we knew how to sympathize with each other.

JINNY AUSTIN: What an awful thing it is.

MRS. AMELIA TILLMAN: Yes, my child. Jealousy has no saving grace, and it only destroys what is always most precious to you. Jinny don't let it destroy your happiness.

JINNY AUSTIN: Mother, if it should, I'll kill myself.

MRS. AMELIA TILLMAN: Don't say such things.

ENTER: MAGGIE

MAGGIE O'RIORDAN: Mr. Tillman is downstairs, madam.

MRS. AMELIA TILLMAN: Tell him to come up.

MAGGIE O'RIORDAN: Yes, madam.

EXIT: MAGGIE

JINNY AUSTIN: Don't tell father anything before I have a chance to tell him myself.

MRS. AMELIA TILLMAN: I don't know that I would tell him at all. He would only advise more cigars.

ENTER: MR. TILLMAN

MR. THOMAS TILLMAN: Are you here?

JINNY AUSTIN: We are, father, and your presence almost completes us. I say almost, because Jack hasn't come home from town yet, and Geoff's heartless enough to stay on Cape Cod fishing.

MR. THOMAS TILLMAN: He's back today.

JINNY AUSTIN: I want to see him.

MR. THOMAS TILLMAN: He was to lunch with Jack. He's going to lodge at the University for a few days.

JINNY AUSTIN: He must dine with us every night.

MR. THOMAS TILLMAN: Jinny. You look as if you've been crying. If you prefer to have secrets from your father, it's all right. I don't begrudge your mother for first place in your affections.

JINNY AUSTIN: Not at all father, with you and mother there's no first place. She will tell you all about it on the way home. Please, mother.

MRS. AMELIA TILLMAN: Very well.

MR. THOMAS TILLMAN: A little "scrap" between you and Jack?

JINNY AUSTIN: Yes, but it's fixed now.

MR. THOMAS TILLMAN: Give your husband these when he comes in.

JINNY AUSTIN: Jack has boxes full of these things.

MR. THOMAS TILLMAN: Never mind. Give him those, from me, with my compliments.

JINNY AUSTIN: Very well.

MR. THOMAS TILLMAN: How are you and Maggie getting on?

JINNY AUSTIN: Splendidly.

MRS. AMELIA TILLMAN: Such a nice girl.

JINNY AUSTIN: Wasn't it odd that Jack was opposed to us having her?

MRS. AMELIA TILLMAN: If we hadn't lent her to you for these past few weeks, you wouldn't have had anybody decent. It's so hard to find good and decent help now.

MR. THOMAS TILLMAN: Did Jack tell you why he didn't want her?

JINNY AUSTIN: I don't know. He just didn't want her. Which makes no sense, I know, but even more last week he talked with her in the library for three-quarters of an hour by my watch. I just don't understand.

MRS. AMELIA TILLMAN: Hmm.

JINNY AUSTIN: It seems she has troubles, too. All single young women with troubles, no matter what class, seem to make a bee line for my husband, even if they have to cross the ocean.

MR. THOMAS TILLMAN: What do you mean?

JINNY AUSTIN: Nothing, but it was about that talk with Maggie that we had our last quarrel.

ENTER: MAGGIE

MAGGIE O'RIORDAN: Mrs. Schram is here. May I --

JINNY AUSTIN: Who?

MAGGIE O'RIORDAN: Mrs. Schram and her son, ma'am. May I show them in?

JINNY AUSTIN: They're in Europe.

MAGGIE O'RIORDAN: They're at the door.

MRS. AMELIA TILLMAN: Are you sure you're not mistaken, Maggie?

MAGGIE O'RIORDAN: Yes ma'am. Even if you could mistake Mrs. Schram, you couldn't mistake Mr. Peter.

JINNY AUSTIN: Ask them to please come up, Maggie.

MAGGIE O'RIORDAN: Yes ma'am.

EXIT: MAGGIE

MR. THOMAS TILLMAN: They only just sailed the other day, didn't they?

MRS. AMELIA TILLMAN: Yes. Weren't they were supposed to be gone all summer for Ruth Chester's health. Why in the world did they come back so soon?

JINNY AUSTIN: I intend to find out.

MR. THOMAS TILLMAN: We must be going, Amelia. What time is it?

JINNY AUSTIN: Six twenty-eight.

MR. THOMAS TILLMAN: We've missed our train.

MRS. AMELIA TILLMAN: We can take the seven-fifteen.

MRS. EULALIA SCHRAM: Jinny. You look like you've seen a ghost.

JINNY AUSTIN: I'm just surprised your back so soon.

MRS. EULALIA SCHRAM: You aren't a bit more surprised than me.

MRS. EULALIA SCHRAM: There goes the half hour. Peter, you must take your powder.

PETER SCHRAM: Mother, I take tablets now. I'm modern.

MRS. EULALIA SCHRAM: Excuse me. I'm dead tired.

JINNY AUSTIN: Have a seat. Will you have some water?

PETER SCHRAM: No, thank you, I've learned to take them *au naturel*, and without much, if any, inconvenience.

MRS. AMELIA TILLMAN: Did you have a bad voyage?

MRS. EULALIA SCHRAM: No, perfectly beautiful.

PETER SCHRAM: Mother.

MRS. EULALIA SCHRAM: Except, of course, for poor Peter. He gets worse every trip. He is so fussy. He can eat "absolutely nothing" -- that is until he finds the candy shops. But it's the Custom House that's wore me out. I was there from twelve to four.

MRS. AMELIA TILLMAN: But you didn't have time to buy anything. You weren't there long enough.

PETER SCHRAM: Mother.

MRS. EULALIA SCHRAM: That's right. But I took plenty of new dresses for the entire summer. Most of them hadn't even been worn. They were determined to make me pay duty on dresses I brought with me.

JINNY AUSTIN: We had to pay awfully for things. I wanted to try and smuggle, but Jack wouldn't let me.

MR. THOMAS TILLMAN: I'm afraid we must go.

MRS. EULALIA SCHRAM: The Inspector had the impudence to finally ask me if I wanted to bring the dresses in as "theatrical properties".

MRS. AMELIA TILLMAN: You must have some gorgeous frocks.

MRS. EULALIA SCHRAM: There are some with sequins. Who did he think I was, Sarah Bernhardt? I have two whole legs. Was he blind?

PETER SCHRAM: Mother.

MR. THOMAS TILLMAN: I don't wish to interrupt this vital political conversation, but, Amelia, if you don't want to miss the seven-fifteen train, also.

MRS. AMELIA TILLMAN: We mustn't do that. Goodbye Eulalia. It's nice to see you again, anyway. Is Ruth better?

MRS. EULALIA SCHRAM: I'm sorry to say I don't think she is. Goodbye.

MRS. AMELIA TILLMAN: You want me to tell your father?

JINNY AUSTIN: Yes, it'll be better that way. It does make him jealous if he thinks I only tell you things and keep secrets from him.

EXIT: MR. AND MRS. TILLMAN

SCENE 2

JINNY AUSTIN: I thought you were abroad indefinitely.

MRS. EULALIA SCHRAM: So did I. I'm just as surprised to be here as you are. You really didn't know we were coming?

JINNY AUSTIN: No. Why should I?

MRS. EULALIA SCHRAM: I don't know. I thought. . .

JINNY AUSTIN: What did you think?

MRS. EULALIA SCHRAM: Nothing, except you must have known we were coming back.

JINNY AUSTIN: Why must I?

MRS. EULALIA SCHRAM: Don't put me into a corner like that.

JINNY AUSTIN: How do you mean "corner"? Why did you return so early?

MRS. EULALIA SCHRAM: Ruth got a cable. She didn't tell me from who, only that she had to return home at once.

JINNY AUSTIN: But her mother's never been better.

PETER SCHRAM: Mother.

MRS. EULALIA SCHRAM: The cable wasn't from her mother.

JINNY AUSTIN: Then, you know who it was from? I see now why you thought I ought to know about it. The cable was from Jack, wasn't it?

MRS. EULALIA SCHRAM: Yes. I looked at it when she was out of the room. Of course, it was sort of by accident that is, I just happened to see ... it ... there ... on the table. You know what I mean. It was wrong, but I couldn't help it.

JINNY AUSTIN: Jack and Ruth are very good friends and he looks after some of her affairs. Her father is dead, which complicates things. So it's natural she needed to talk with Jack.

PETER SCHRAM: Mother.

MRS. EULALIA SCHRAM: What is it?

PETER SCHRAM: I don't have my before-dinner tablets.

MRS. EULALIA SCHRAM: Look carefully.

PETER SCHRAM: Soda mints. Alkali powders. Charcoal tablets. Dr. Man's Positive Cure. Bicarbonate soda.

MRS. EULALIA SCHRAM: Your other side pocket.

PETER SCHRAM: That's my saccharine and my Winslow tablets. We'll have to go, mother. I've left them home.

MRS. EULALIA SCHRAM: I suppose we must be going. Goodbye Jinny.

PETER SCHRAM: Wait. I forgot my hip pocket. Here they are.

MRS. EULALIA SCHRAM: We must go all the same. Sometimes I think he takes too many pills.

JINNY AUSTIN: I should think so. Peter, you ought to diet and exercise.

PETER SCHRAM: I can't. I've tried and I lose my appetite right away.

MRS. EULALIA SCHRAM: How long will you be in town?

JINNY AUSTIN: I don't know, several weeks, I imagine. Jack came home on some business, you know, and I don't think it's settled yet. Au revoir.

PETER SCHRAM: You know you mustn't drink water with your meals. I only drink champagne. Goodbye. I'll meet you downstairs mother.

EXIT: PETER

MRS. EULALIA SCHRAM: I'm awfully ashamed of myself, and I hope I haven't made any trouble or fuss with my meddling. Don't let me…

JINNY AUSTIN: No, of course not.

MRS. EULALIA SCHRAM: Thank you, but all the same. Goodbye.

EXIT: MRS. SCHRAM

JINNY AUSTIN: Well.

SCENE 3

JINNY AUSTIN: Where's that telegram that came a little while ago? Of course, it's from her, saying that she's arrived. That's the trouble with telegrams. The address doesn't give the handwriting away. She must have sent it from the dock. Couldn't even wait till she was home. Nearly seven already, and no sign of him, and we must still dress, dine, and get ready for the theater. Did he go down there to meet her? If he cabled her to come back, she must have cabled back what boat she'd take. He must have known when the boat was to arrive. But no other telegram has come for Jack. What am I thinking? She sent that one to his office today. She was afraid he might have left before this one could get there, so she risked it here. Why am I prattling on like this to myself out loud? It's nothing. Jack will explain once more that he can't explain, but that Ruth has "troubles," and I'll believe him again. But I won't. He promised me she should stay in Europe for the summer. He's with her now. Nothing ever kept him half as late downtown before. What a fool I am.

ENTER: GEOFF

JINNY AUSTIN: Geoff. Why didn't you come straight back to New York when you heard I was home.

GEOFF TILLMAN: I couldn't. I'm sorry. How are you?

JINNY AUSTIN: I'm doing well. I don't know. Was there a pretty girl, Geoff?

GEOFF TILLMAN: Hasn't Jack come back yet?

JINNY AUSTIN: "Come back" from where?

GEOFF TILLMAN: Brooklyn.

JINNY AUSTIN: Brooklyn? He told me he was at his Manhattan office today. Why did he go there?

GEOFF TILLMAN: I don't know.

JINNY AUSTIN: You do.

GEOFF TILLMAN: No really, I....

JINNY AUSTIN: It's something to be concealed from me. Right? What are you hiding from me?

GEOFF TILLMAN: Drop it, Jinny. Drop the subject. I thought he said he was going to Brooklyn. I was mistaken.

JINNY AUSTIN: One is so apt to think, just casually, that every one's going to Brooklyn. Of course, it's Brooklyn. So you're against me, too? You're going to protect Jack at my expense?

GEOFF TILLMAN: Jinny.

ENTER: JACK

JINNY AUSTIN: It's after seven.

JACK AUSTIN: Is it? Have you been waiting long, Geoff?

GEOFF TILLMAN: No, I've only just arrived.

JINNY AUSTIN: I've been waiting.

JACK AUSTIN: I'm sorry, but it couldn't be helped.

JINNY AUSTIN: You didn't tell me you were going to Brooklyn.

JACK AUSTIN: It must have escaped my mind.

JINNY AUSTIN: That's very likely. Going to Brooklyn is the sort of thing one talks about and dreads for days.

JACK AUSTIN: That will bear postponement, and my conversation with Geoff won't. Will you please leave us together here for a while?

JINNY AUSTIN: And what about the theater?

JACK AUSTIN: What theater?

JINNY AUSTIN: You forgot my little birthday party for you?

JACK AUSTIN: I did. I'm awfully sorry. I've got a lot on my mind today.

JINNY AUSTIN: Yes I know you have. I'll leave you two alone to your business. You can trust Geoff to keep your secrets.

JACK AUSTIN: What did you tell her? I can tell you her behavior lies largely on your already overcrowded shoulders. You have to be extra careful of what and how you say things to her.

GEOFF TILLMAN: I know. I know.

JACK AUSTIN: Here, don't cry. You've got to be strong. You've no use nor time for crying. I've had another long interview with the Brooklyn minister.

GEOFF TILLMAN: And?

JACK AUSTIN: We both know he's doing wrong to keep silent, but he will. He does wish I hadn't told him because he doesn't think he would have recognized your name when the divorce was printed in the papers.

GEOFF TILLMAN: That's what I told you.

JACK AUSTIN: You only argued that for fear I'd insist that you go to him yourself. But you know it was a risk we couldn't afford to run. I explained everything to him. I explained how such a fine, sweet girl would suffer if he did expose you. And I gave him my word you would be remarried to Ruth once the divorce settled. It's wrong, but we both hope the end justifies the means. That removes difficulty number two.

GEOFF TILLMAN: What about the first one? You're sure about Maggie?

JACK AUSTIN: She's signed a paper. She realizes you'll never live with her. It's pathetic. She loves you … as well as Ruth, too. Maggie loves you so much she'll give you your freedom. Good Lord, what is it about weak men that win women? What is it in you? That made two women love you, to such a self-sacrificing extent? The settlement agreement arranges for Maggie to have six hundred dollars a year.

GEOFF TILLMAN: Six hundred dollars? Where'll I get it?

JACK AUSTIN: We'll talk about that when the time comes. Now the most important, the most painful task of all must be done. And you must do it alone. Not me this time, but you.

GEOFF TILLMAN: What?

JACK AUSTIN: Ruth Chester arrived back from Europe this morning.

GEOFF TILLMAN: No.

JACK AUSTIN: The moment Maggie signed the agreement I cabled Ruth to return. You can't go to South Dakota and start divorce proceedings without telling her the whole truth first. Do you really want her to find it in the newspapers?

GEOFF TILLMAN: And you want me to tell her?

JACK AUSTIN: Yes. Today. And tomorrow you start west.

GEOFF TILLMAN: I can't.

JACK AUSTIN: You've got to.

GEOFF TILLMAN: I'd rather shoot myself. Can't you understand?

JACK AUSTIN: That would be the easiest course out of it, and the most cowardly.

GEOFF TILLMAN: I'll lose her. She'll hate me. How couldn't she? At least at first. Maybe she will reconcile it and love me as she once did. Maybe she'll forgive me?

JACK AUSTIN: You must brace yourself for the worst. I don't deny that you will have to go through a terrible degradation with her, but that is nothing compared with what you deserve. If you tell her, at least the humiliation is secret, locked there between you two. If you send someone else, you make a spectacle of her humiliation. To let a third in as witness to this is betrayal. It's insulting her again. Don't you see?

GEOFF TILLMAN: Yes, I see. I'll tell her.

JACK AUSTIN: Don't waver, make up your mind and do it. Come.

GEOFF TILLMAN: And Jinny?

JACK AUSTIN: She'll come round all right. She always does.

GEOFF TILLMAN: And she doesn't suspect?

JACK AUSTIN: Not the slightest.

GEOFF TILLMAN: Need she?

JACK AUSTIN: The worst? No, never.

GEOFF TILLMAN: You give me your word?

JACK AUSTIN: Yes. I know how much she loves you. If it had been up to me she wouldn't know anything. Because I've had to be discreet and secretive about all this, it's made us some ugly scenes. It really ignited her jealous nature. And as soon as your situation is fixed, we'll have no excuse to fight anymore, and we can get on with our married life.

GEOFF TILLMAN: Then I shall go to bed tonight with the respect of at least two women. Even if I lose the respect and love of the one woman who is… Jack, how do I to stand in front of her… and watch her pain?

JACK AUSTIN: The one hope you have of forgiveness, is in your strength of telling her the whole truth.

EXIT: GEOFF

SCENE 4

JACK AUSTIN: Jinny, Geoff's left. What are you doing?

JINNY AUSTIN: [OFFSTAGE] Waiting till you have the leisure to receive me.

ENTER: JINNY

JINNY AUSTIN: I didn't care to go downstairs for dinner, so I had a tray sent up. Maggie brought something for you, too. Would you like it now?

JACK AUSTIN: I do feel a little hungry.

JINNY AUSTIN: Bring in the tray for Mr. Austin, Maggie.

MAGGIE O'RIORDAN: [OFFSTAGE] Yes ma'am.

ENTER: MAGGIE

JINNY AUSTIN: What did Geoff want? He didn't even stop to see me on his way out. Maybe it's not too late to go to the theater after all.

JACK AUSTIN: I am hungry.

JINNY AUSTIN: Lamb chops. This is the third time this week. I must talk with cook.

JACK AUSTIN: But they are very good. I'll tell you what it is, travelling is great sport, but one gets tired of hotels. And to quote a somewhat familiar refrain, [SINGS] "There's no place like home." Do you have a headache?

JINNY AUSTIN: No.

JACK AUSTIN: That's a good thing, and I hope you are not as disappointed as I am about the theater. We'll celebrate tomorrow. I'll get the tickets.

JINNY AUSTIN: Why did you go to Brooklyn?

JACK AUSTIN: It was private business.

JINNY AUSTIN: That's the best answer you can give me?

JACK AUSTIN: It's the only answer.

JINNY AUSTIN: When you are finished, I have something for you.

JACK AUSTIN: What?

JINNY AUSTIN: I'll give it to you when you've finished.

JACK AUSTIN: I'm done. What's that?

[JINNY GIVES JACK THE TELEGRAM]

[JINNY RINGS THE SERVANTS BELL]

JACK AUSTIN: When did this come?

JINNY AUSTIN: This afternoon.

JACK AUSTIN: Why didn't Maggie give it to me when I came in?

JINNY AUSTIN: I kept it to have the pleasure of giving it to you myself. It's from Ruth Chester.

JACK AUSTIN: How do you know?

JINNY AUSTIN: I didn't open it. But I know. When I held it in my hand it burnt my fingers.

ENTER: MAGGIE

JINNY AUSTIN: Maggie.

MAGGIE: Yes, ma'am?

JINNY AUSTIN: Please take away the tray.

MAGGIE O'RIORDAN: Yes ma'am.

EXIT: MAGGIE

JINNY AUSTIN: May I read it?

JACK AUSTIN: If you wish.

JINNY AUSTIN: I do.

JACK AUSTIN: When you behave like this it's impossible for me to feel any trust toward you.

JINNY AUSTIN: And how do you think I feel when I read this?

"Arrived safely. Stop. Please let me see you before the day goes. Stop. Ruth." Ruth.

JACK AUSTIN: Don't work my nerves tonight. I've been through a great deal today.

JINNY AUSTIN: I've been through a great deal for many a day now too. And I want the truth about this. It's all very well for you to spare her by not telling me what this mysterious trouble is about. You've been hoodwinking me ever since we were married. But now you've got to choose between sparing her and sparing me.

JACK AUSTIN: Be careful, don't work my nerves, Jinny.

JINNY AUSTIN: It's your turn to be careful. Why did you marry me for if you loved Ruth?

JACK AUSTIN: Jinny.

JINNY AUSTIN: You gave me your word of honor that she would stay abroad indefinitely.

JACK AUSTIN: No. I said I understood she was going to stay some time indefinitely.

JINNY AUSTIN: It's the same thing, and here she is back, practically the moment we are.

JACK AUSTIN: I can't control Ruth's movements. I couldn't foresee when she would come back. In Rome she told me she would stay on.

JINNY AUSTIN: That's what I wanted to see. If you really would lie to me. Lie to my face.

JACK AUSTIN: What do you mean?

JINNY AUSTIN: Liar. You sent for Ruth to come back. You tried to deceive me about it. And if you tell me a lie about one thing, you'll tell me a lie about another, and I don't believe one word of all your explanations about the intrigue between you and Ruth Chester.

JACK AUSTIN: Sit down.

JINNY AUSTIN: Why did you send for Ruth Chester? Why is she back?

JACK AUSTIN: I told you before, I'm helping her.

JINNY AUSTIN: Ruth.

JACK AUSTIN: I'm helping her with a great and serious problem.

JINNY AUSTIN: Why did you send for her to come back? What's her problem?

JACK AUSTIN: I've told you before it's confidential.

JINNY AUSTIN: You can't tell me? Or you won't? And you haven't even the face to tell another lie about it.

JACK AUSTIN: If you say another word, I shall hate you. If you won't control yourself ... You have insulted my love for you tonight as you've never done before. You've struck at my own ideal of you. You've almost done, in a word, what I warned you... you are... killing the love I have for you.

JINNY AUSTIN: Jack.

JACK AUSTIN: I mean it. Leave me alone.

JINNY AUSTIN: That...that you... you don't love me?

JACK AUSTIN: That is not what I said. Don't touch me. But I tell you now that since I first began to care for you, never have I loved you so little as I do tonight.

JINNY AUSTIN: And suppose I tell you it is your own fault because you haven't treated me....

JACK AUSTIN: Like a child instead of a woman.

JINNY AUSTIN: No, because you've kept part of yourself from me, and that part you've given to . . .

JACK AUSTIN: For God's sake, stop. Do you want a permanent rift between us? Can't you see I'm telling you the truth? I've had enough for tonight. If you keep on it'll rob me of every bit of love I have for you. You've already changed my image of you.

JINNY AUSTIN: "Already." No, no, don't say that. What have I done?

JACK AUSTIN: It would be wiser for both of us if we went out somewhere tonight. Seperate.

JINNY AUSTIN: No, I couldn't go out feeling this way. I've hurt you. Why do I do it? Why can't I help myself?

JACK AUSTIN: One more scene tonight will finish things for us.

JINNY AUSTIN: Don't say it. Please forgive me, I hate myself. I'm so ashamed of myself. I know I've disappointed you awfully. You did idolize me. I knew it when you married me, but I told you then I wasn't worth your love, didn't I? I never pretended to be worthy of you. I always knew I wasn't. It's true. It's only too awfully true. But do you remember how you answered me then, when I told you I wasn't worth your loving me?

JACK AUSTIN: Apparently you aren't worth my love or you'd trust me.

JINNY AUSTIN: You took me in your arms and held me so I couldn't have got away if I'd wanted to, which I didn't, and stopped the words on my lips with your kisses. How I wish you'd answer me that way now.

JACK AUSTIN: Whose fault is it?

JINNY AUSTIN: Mine. Mine. I know it. You don't know it one-half so well as I do. I love you better than anything in the world. I love everything about you. I love the turn of your head, the tender touch of your hand, the smallest word that comes from your lips, and the thoughts that your forehead hides. And yet, try as hard as I can, these mad fits take hold of me. I'd willingly die to save you pain. I, I, I hurt and wounded you past all bearing. It doesn't make any difference that I suffer. I should. I deserve it. You don't. No. I know
. . .

JACK AUSTIN: No, Jinny. It's not as bad as that. I saw you as a goddess, like the Athena statue in Rome. So big and full of life. I thought you were stronger .. more noble … wiser.

JINNY AUSTIN: Yes, it's true. I'm small, I'm weak. I want to be strong, to be noble, too. But I'm not. I'm as weak as water, that's always boiling over. I want to be Brunhilde, but I'm only Frou-Frou. Yes, I'm little and weak. I love you. I love you. Forgive me?

JACK AUSTIN: Yes.

JINNY AUSTIN: You don't mind me sitting here?

JACK AUSTIN: No.

JINNY AUSTIN: Thank you, thank you, I know I don't deserve it. I don't deserve it. I don't deserve it. You forgive me? But still. I see it in your face, you don't love me the same. And you look tired.

JACK AUSTIN: I am tired.

JINNY AUSTIN: Are you happy?

JACK AUSTIN: Not quite.

JINNY AUSTIN: I wish I could make you happy. Make you love me the old way. You used to smile a little when you looked at me Jack. You don't anymore. Please love me as much as you ever you did. What time is it?

JACK AUSTIN: Nearly nine.

JINNY AUSTIN: I suppose it is too late for me to dress and for us to go to the theater?

JACK AUSTIN: I'm too tired.

JINNY AUSTIN: Then you shall have your theater at home.

JACK AUSTIN: I don't understand.

JINNY AUSTIN: Just wait till I bathe my face and eyes a little. I feel rather bleary. I'll be right back. I'll make you smile yet and make you kiss me of your own accord tonight you'll see.

EXIT: JINNY

SFX: FOOTSTEPS GOING UP THE STAIRS

JACK AUSTIN: [WRITING A LETTER]

JINNY AUSTIN: [OFFSTAGE] Are you ready?

JACK AUSTIN: Yes.

JINNY AUSTIN: [OFFSTAGE] In your orchestra seat?

JACK AUSTIN: Yes.

JINNY AUSTIN: [OFFSTAGE] What will you have, tragedy or comedy?

JACK AUSTIN: Shall we begin with tragedy?

JINNY AUSTIN: All right. Curtain in five.

JACK AUSTIN: Thank you five. [WRITING]

SFX: FOOTSTEPS COMING DOWN THE STAIRS

ENTER: JINNY

JINNY AUSTIN: Excuse me one minute while I set the stage. Ophelia goes
down to the river. She is distraught that Hamlet ignores her and that her
father is dead. Life is chaotic and dangerous. So she carries daisies and
slowly goes into the deepest part of the water.

They bore him barefaced on the bier,
Hey no nonny, nonny, hey nonny
And on his grave rained many a tear. —
Fare you well, my dove!

You must sing '*Down a-down, and you call him a-down-a.*' How the wheel
becomes it! It is the false steward that stole his master's daughter. There's
rosemary, that's for remembrance. Pray love, remember. And there is
pansies, that's for thoughts. There's fennel for you, and columbines. There's
rue for you and here's some for me. We may call it herb of grace of Sundays.
You must wear your rue with a difference. There's a daisy. I would give you
some violets, but they withered all when my father died. They say he made
a good end.

For bonny sweet Robin is all my joy.
And will he not come again?
And will he not come again?
No, no, he is dead,
Go to thy death-bed,
He never will come again.
His beard was as white as snow,
All flaxen was his poll.
He is gone, he is gone,
And we cast away moan.
God ha' mercy on his soul.

And of all Christian souls, I pray God. God be with ye.

[Or Sing the song *Tell Me Pretty Daisy* (1895) from Hamlet II, a burlesque of the Bard's play music by Homer Tourjée and book by Henry Grattan Donnelly.

Verse:

Aweary is the heart of tender maiden,
When silent sorrow sits within her breast,
Adreary are the days with longing laden,
With longing for the love to make her blest.

There's naught of joy in all the summer's gladness,
There's naught of peace in music's melody,
There's naught in all of life except its sadness,
The broken voice sings softly plaintively.

Chorus:

Tell me pretty petals is my lover true?
Oh tell me pretty daisy I may trust in you;
Tell me does my lover love fond and faithfully?
Oh tell me does my lover love, loves my love but me?]

JACK AUSTIN: I'm sure we couldn't have seen better at the theater.

JINNY AUSTIN: You're yourself again. Darling. Come. Come. Come to the player piano and you shall have the *Floradora* sextette. It's in there already. I heard mother struggling with it this morning.

[JACK PLAYS THE SEXTETTE FROM *FLORADORA*.]

JINNY AUSTIN: Now. Ready?

JACK AUSTIN: But I can't see you and play at the same time. I don't like it.

JINNY AUSTIN: You want to see me, don't you?

JACK AUSTIN: Of course, I do.

JINNY AUSTIN: Then turn round. Jack. You're smiling again.

JACK AUSTIN: Yes. Is the theater finished?

JINNY AUSTIN: No, only the first act. I need an intermission.

SFX: [KNOCKING]

[JACK STOPS PLAYING]

JINNY AUSTIN: Hang it.

SFX: [KNOCKING]

JINNY AUSTIN: Don't answer it. We don't have to be available and we haven't half made up yet.

SFX: [KNOCKING]

JACK AUSTIN: But we must answer it.

JINNY AUSTIN: I don't see why. Let her knock till she goes away.

JACK AUSTIN: Come in.

ENTER: MAGGIE

SCENE 5

JINNY AUSTIN: What is it, Maggie?

MAGGIE O'RIORDAN: A note from Miss Chester, ma'am. She's downstairs.

JINNY AUSTIN: For me?

MAGGIE O'RIORDAN: No, ma'am. I think she said it was for Mr. Austin.

JINNY AUSTIN: You may wait outside Maggie.

MAGGIE O'RIORDAN: Yes, ma'am.

EXIT: MAGGIE

JINNY AUSTIN: I now see why you were so anxious to let Maggie in. Perhaps you were expecting this. Is she in on it too?

JACK AUSTIN: Jinny. Come, I'll give you a kiss for the letter.

JINNY AUSTIN: No, thank you, I don't want kisses from you in exchange for letters from Ruth Chester. Ok. Kiss me. I won't be jealous. I won't be. See, I'm not jealous a bit. Read your old letter.

[JINNY FINDS THE LETTER JACK JUST WROTE RUTH.]

JINNY AUSTIN: Jack.

JACK AUSTIN: What is it?

JINNY AUSTIN: Nothing. May I read the letter in your hand?

JACK AUSTIN: Now look here, Jinny, I always let you read everything, don't I?

JINNY AUSTIN: Yes. Give it to me.

JACK AUSTIN: Please prove that you are turning over a new leaf, and that you trust me, and don't ask to see this letter.

JINNY AUSTIN: But I am.

JACK AUSTIN: I must refuse.

JINNY AUSTIN: What? Is it even more compromising than your letter to her?

JACK AUSTIN: What letter?

JINNY AUSTIN: The one laying open on your desk. Here. A letter that tells me that I've a right to be jealous. I've been right all along. I've been a fool too.

JACK AUSTIN: Is that all.

JINNY AUSTIN: "Is that all." Isn't that enough? You and Ruth want to get rid of me.

JACK AUSTIN: If it tells you that, the letter lies. Give it to me.

JINNY AUSTIN: No. I'll read it to you.

"The satisfaction of the visit to Brooklyn prevents me from being disappointed at having missed your telegram till too late to go to your house tonight."

So, you both went to Brooklyn, did you, and that's why you came back too late to go to the theater with me? You cheat. Why don't you answer me? Why don't you say something?

JACK AUSTIN: Because if I speak as I feel, I'm afraid I'll regret it.

JINNY AUSTIN: You don't deny it?

JACK AUSTIN: Yes.

JINNY AUSTIN: There's more in the letter.

JACK AUSTIN: Don't you see what you're doing?

JINNY AUSTIN: Yes, I'm getting to the truth at last.

"My heart aches for the blow you must have this evening. The man who loves you."

JACK AUSTIN: Don't read any more. You're insane.

JINNY AUSTIN: I don't need the letter. The words are burning in here.

"The man who loves you isn't bad, only weak. However, I feel once we can shake off the burden of this present marriage"

You... you ... to say that ...

"you will never have cause to complain of him again. So far, I have been able to keep Jinny in perfect ignorance, but I feel the blow must fall upon her now "

JACK AUSTIN: Can I explain?

JINNY AUSTIN: You don't have to. I discovered it myself.

JACK AUSTIN: No...no.

SFX: KNOCK AT DOOR

JACK AUSTIN: Come in.

ENTER: MAGGIE

MAGGIE O'RIORDAN: Please, sir, Miss Chester came upstairs and made me knock again to see if there was an answer and if you will see her now.

JINNY AUSTIN: Yes. Maggie, show her in.

JACK AUSTIN: No. What are you doing? I'll see Miss Chester tomorrow, Maggie.

JINNY AUSTIN: No. Ruth.

RUTH CHESTER: [OFFSTAGE] Yes? May I come?

JINNY AUSTIN: Come in.

ENTER: RUTH

RUTH CHESTER: Jinny. What is it? Why are you looking at me like that?

JACK AUSTIN: She doesn't know, but she thinks she knows.

JINNY AUSTIN: That's a lie. I know everything. Ruth, I know why you followed my husband to Rome. I know why he sent for you to come here. I know that you were in Brooklyn together this afternoon. And I know that you plan to get rid of me to marry each other.

RUTH CHESTER: No. No. No. No.

JINNY AUSTIN: You lie too? I won't keep you waiting very long. You've stolen my husband from me, so take him. I won't share him with any woman. He's yours now, and I'll soon be out of your way.

JACK AUSTIN: Jinny.

RUTH CHESTER: She must be told the truth.

JINNY AUSTIN: Now you'll make up your story, will you? It's useless, I've read the letter he wrote to you tonight that gives the whole thing away.

RUTH CHESTER: Your husband went to Brooklyn without me, as your brother will tell you, to see the pastor who married me, or thought he married me to Geoff three months ago. That marriage was illegal because your brother was already married. Jack went to the pastor this afternoon and secured his

71

silence about the Brooklyn marriage, to prevent a charge of bigamy against your brother.

JACK AUSTIN: Geoff is not at your house?

RUTH CHESTER: No, he left when I came on here. As I wrote you in the note, I was too stunned by what he told me to answer then. I wanted a word of advice with you before I made my decision. I knew what I thought was my marriage to your brother must be kept secret, but I didn't know why. This was my problem which I selfishly laid on your husband's shoulders. Hoping he might help me. Jack only learned the whole truth when we met that day in Rome. I learned today that I am not honestly your brother's wife. He told me because divorce proceedings will begin in South Dakota to break his first marriage. A marriage to your servant Maggie.

MAGGIE: I was pregnant.

RUTH CHESTER: Your husband kept Geoff's secret from you to spare me, and above all to spare you the knowledge of your brother's sin. You have well repaid him. I've made my decision. I can't marry Geoff. I never will marry Geoff and I don't want to ever see his face again. Sorry Jinny. He betrayed me. I hate him. You can tell him that for me. And you can have him.

EXIT: RUTH

EXIT: MAGGIE

JINNY AUSTIN: Can you forgive me? Can you? I'm mad. You know I don't know what I do. I love you; I love you. Forgive me.

JACK AUSTIN: Never.

JINNY AUSTIN: Where are you going?

JACK AUSTIN: I'm leaving.

JINNY AUSTIN: If you leave me, I'll not bear it. I'll kill myself. I warn you.

JACK AUSTIN: Goodbye.

JINNY AUSTIN: No. Where are you going?

JACK AUSTIN: I'm leaving.

JINNY AUSTIN: For good?

JACK AUSTIN: For good.

EXIT: JACK

JINNY AUSTIN: Jack, Jack, Jack. What have I done? Jack

CURTAIN

PROPERTY LIST

ACT 1-Tillman's House. Bronx, New York.
Side tables with wedding flowers.
Chairs.
Gaslight sconces.
Wrapped present.
A Door.

ACT II-A museum in Europe or the Vatican specifically.
An image of Apollo Belvedere (with or without fig leaf)
Baedeker Travel Guidebook.
Letters.
Candy.
Pills and powders.

ACT III-Austin's House. Queens, New York
Book by Guy de Maupassant.
Electric lights.
Telegrams.
Letters.

ORIGINAL CAST
CLYDE FITCH: THE GIRL WITH THE GREEN EYES,
A Play In Four Acts

To CLARA BLOODGOOD Good Friend and Ideal Interpreter of Jinny.

Originally produced under the management of Charles Frohman at the
Savoy Theater, New York, on the December 25, 1902 (which ran for
108 performances) with the following cast:

Jinny Austin	Miss Clara Bloodgood
Mr. Tillman	Mr. Charles Abbott
Mrs. Tillman	Mrs. Harriet Otis Dellenbaugh
Geoffrey Tillman	Mr. John M. Albaugh, Jr.
Susie	Miss Edith Taliaferro
Miss Ruth Chester	Miss Lucille Flaven
Miss Grace Dane	Miss Mary Blyth
Miss Belle Westing	Miss Helena Otis
Miss Gertrude Wood	Miss Felice Morris
Maggie	Miss Lucile Watson
Housemaid	Miss Angela Keir
Butler	Mr. Gardner Jenkins
Footman	Mr. Walter Dickinson
John Austin	Mr. Robert Drouet
Mrs. Cullingham	Mrs. McKee Rankin
Peter Cullingham	Mr. Harry E. Asmus
Mrs. Lopp	Miss Ellen Rowland
Carrie	Miss Clara B. Hunter
A French Couple	Mr. Henry De Barry
	Miss Louise Delmar
A German Couple	Mr. J. R. Cooley
	Miss Elsa Ganett
A Guide	Mr. Frank Brownlee
A Driver	Mr. Lou W. Carter
	Miss Elizabeth French
A Group of Tourists	Miss Gertrude Bindley
	Miss Myrtle Lane

Tell Me Pretty Daisy

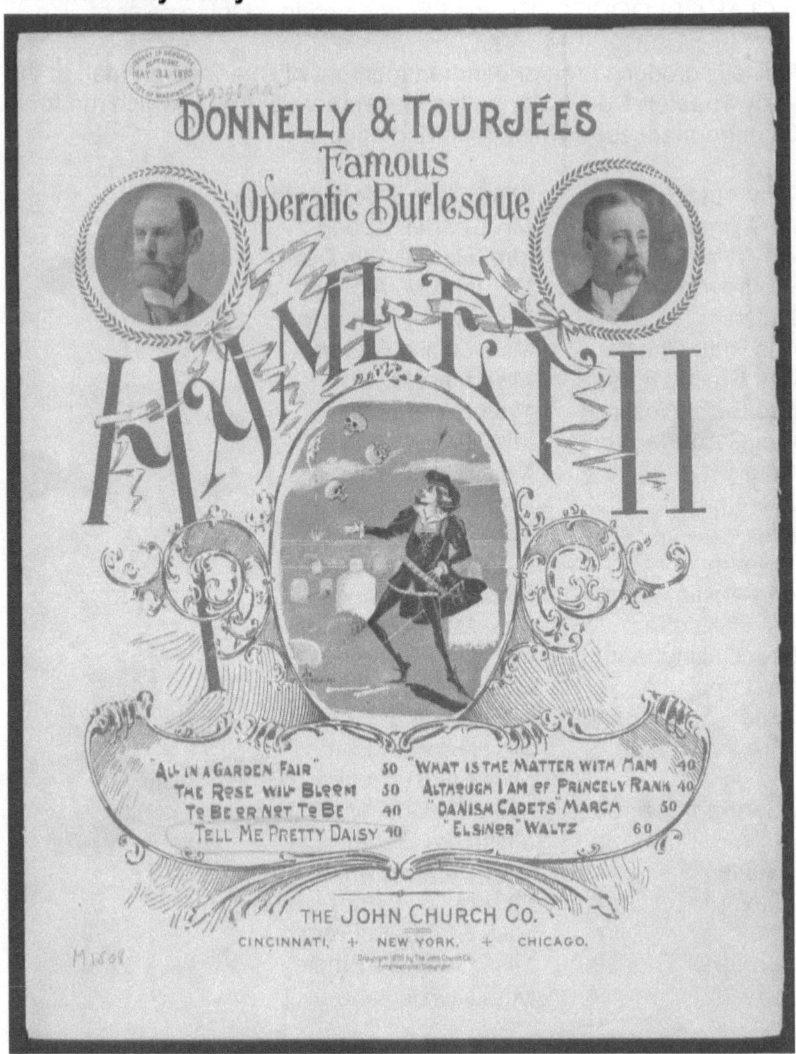

TELL ME PRETTY DAISY.

la - den With long - ing for the love to make her
blest.......... There's naught of joy in all the summer's glad-ness There's
naught of peace in mu-sic's mel - o - dy, There's naught in all of life ex-cept-its
sad - ness, The bro-ken voice sings soft and plaintive - ly.
rall.

dolce.
Tempo di valse.
Tell me pret - ty pet - - als is my lov-er true?_____ Oh
tell me pret - ty dai - - sy I may trust to you;_____
Tell me does my lov-er love fond and faith - ful - ly?_____ Oh
tell me does my lov - er love, loves my love but me?_____

Tell Me Pretty Maiden.

English Girls and Clerks.

By LESLIE STUART.

Copyright MCM by Francis, Day & Hunter.

Kind sir, their
Dear maid they
tell me, pret-ty maid-en, What these ver-y sim-ple girl-ies do. Then
tell me, gen-tle sir, The things these ver-y rak-ish fel-lows do. Then
man-ners are per-fec-tion, And the op-po-site of mine.
flirt with girls too free-ly And it's not the same girl twice.
tell me, maid-en, what the girl - - ies do. Then take a lit-tle
tell me, tell me what these fel - - lows do, Then take me 'round and
I may love
I nev-er in-tro-
walk with me, And then I can see What a most par-tic-u-lar girl should be.
let them show for an hour or so How far such fel-lows can real-ly__ go.

you too well to let you go And flirt with those at home, you know,
duce them to a girl I in-tend To be my most par - tic-u - lar friend
Well,
I
It's
It's
don't mind, lit - tle girl You'll see I'll on - ly want but
won't mind, what they do No man would ev - er flirt with
not quite fair to them If you told them that you were
not worth risk- ing it I know with them you won't a
you.
me.
I
I

true.
gree.
What would you say if I said I liked you well?
Of course I will try, for we're do-ing ver-y well?
won't care a pin for your sis-ters if you love me.
don't want to know them if you will do the flirt-ing.
I'd
I'll
On bend-ed knee!
On bend-ed knee!
If
If
vow to you
vow to you
On bend-ed knee!
On bend-ed knee!
I loved you, would you tell me what I ought to do To keep you
I loved you, would you tell me what I ought to do To keep you
p

all mine a-lone, to al - ways be true to me? If
all mine a-lone, to al - ways be true to me? If
I loved you, would it be a sil-ly thing to do? For I
I loved you, would it be a sil-ly thing to do? For I
must love some one, Yes, I
must love some one, Yes, I
Then why not me?
Then why not me?

must love some one, real - ly And it might as well be you!
must love some one, real - ly And it might as well be you!
p
p
p

NOTES

NOTES

NOTES

NOTES

www.ingramcontent.com/pod-product-compliance
Lightning Source LLC
Chambersburg PA
CBHW020744160726
47993CB00006B/2603